# remember love

rumi ~ hafiz ~ kabir ~ mirabai ~ buson ~ ho xuan huong

deirdre burton (images)
tom davis (retranslations)

Strange Shadows
128d Oxford Road
Birmingham

Published by Strange Shadows 2010
www.strangeshadows.co.uk
Copyright © Strange Shadows 2010

ISBN 978-0-9558831-1-8

Copyright 2010 by the authors of this book (Deirdre Burton and Tom Davis). The authors retain sole copyright to their contributions to this book. The Blurb-provided layout designs and graphic elements are copyright Blurb Inc., 2009. This book was created using the Blurb creative publishing service.

blurb.com

For Elizabeth Burridge, whose beautiful wild spirit is in all of these poems.

spring fever

Today, look: another day. Waking, wide open,
afraid. Don't dive into the library,
into yet another book! Reach for your guitar,
let love, let beauty, be what it is we do:
you don't have to fly abroad, in order to kneel
and kiss the tarmac!

The breeze at dawn has secrets to tell you.
Don't go back to sleep.
You must ask for what you really want.
Don't go back to sleep.
People are going in and out of the door
where the two worlds touch.
The door is right there, look, it's wide open!
Don't go back to sleep.

Rumi

secrets to
tell you

be free

In the end you disappeared, gone beyond sight;
strange, the path you took, leaving this world;
strange how the beat of your wings destroyed the cage
and you flew to the world of the soul.

You were a nightingale, drunk amidst the owl music,
drunk with the music of joy.
When the scent of the rose garden reached you
you were gone.

Now that you are the sun, what good is a crown?
And how do you tie your belt
now that your body is air?
You were rain from heaven
that fell on this dry earth.

Be silent. Be free
of all the pain of speech.
Now, now you can rest
in the arms of the Beloved.

Rumi

BE SILENT
BE FREE

I shall be that

I was stone; I died
and became a rose
and died, and became
a butterfly. And died
and found myself to be
human. No fear,
no lessening in death.
Next time, perhaps,
an angel. And next, perhaps
what cannot be imagined:
I shall be that.

Rumi

be that

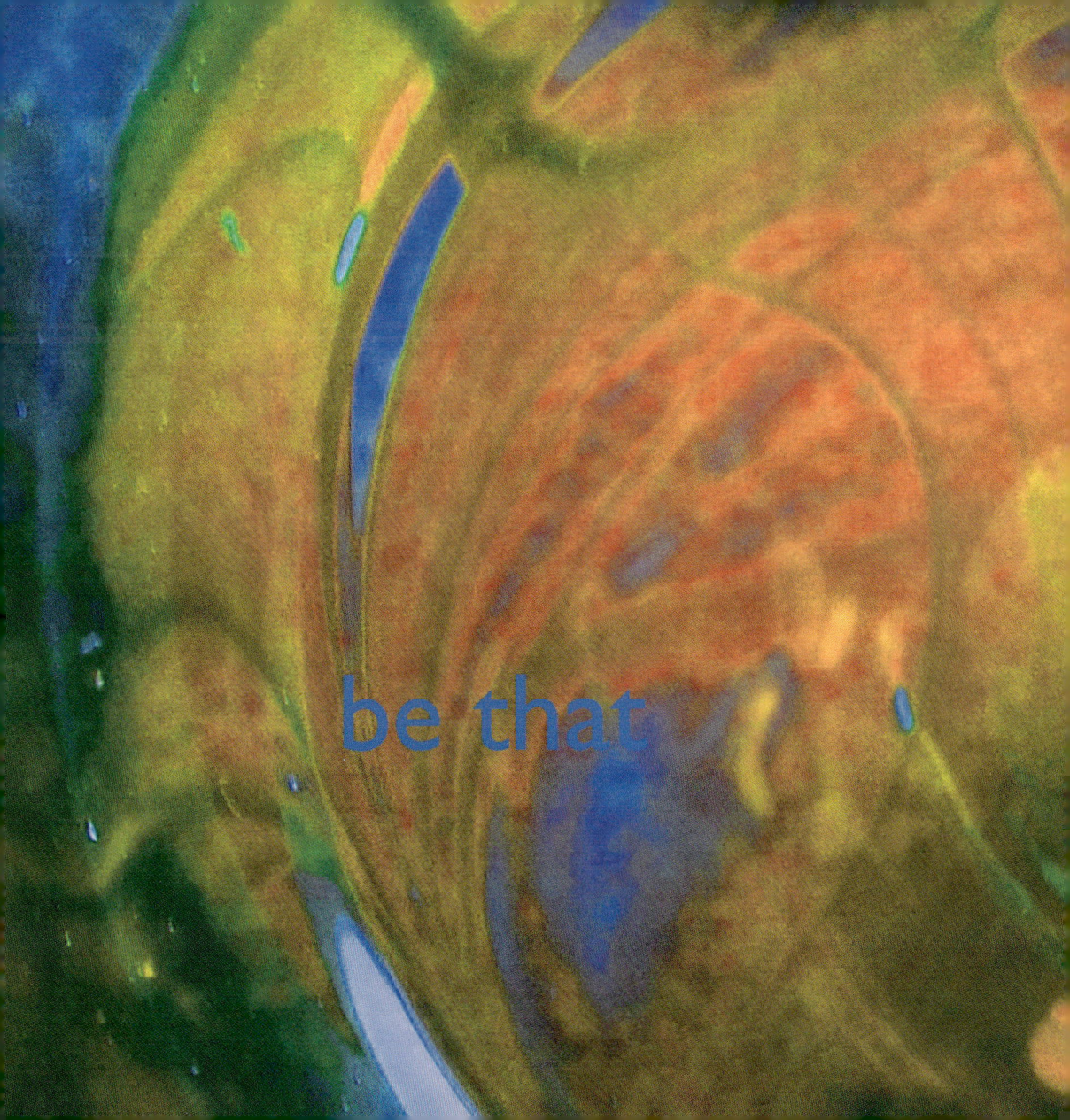

my sweet crushed angel

You didn't dance so badly, my dear, my love:
not easy to keep the beat with beauty itself.
You moved like an angel, my sweet, crushed angel,
getting that near to God.

Hard to follow, those moves of His,
are they not, sweetheart, my heart?
And His musicians, well: how many can hear them at all?
OK, so the music has stopped, for a while;
so, tonight, it costs just too much to get down with God.

But Hafiz knows the way God works.
Have patience, angel, He will feel your desire,
and there He will be: for you.
You didn't dance so badly, my dear, my heart:
not easy, you know, to embrace the unbearable.
You moved like an angel,
O my sweet,
my sweet crushed angel.

Hafiz

hear them

in every meeting

In every meeting, in any chance encounter,
on the street, say,
there is a shining,
an elegance, an arising:

a jewel. Today, I thought it through: that beauty
is the presence, right here
in all our muddled love
of a light in which its clay
is brighter than fire:

the Friend.
I asked: "Is there a way to you,
a ladder?"
"Your head is the ladder.
Bring it down under your feet."

The mind, this spin
of things, becomes
a universe of stars, but only when
you step up on it, to rise.

Rumi

brighter
than
fire

I long to kiss you.

I long to kiss you.
The price of kissing is your life.
Hearing this, love runs up to me, shouting:
'What a bargain, buy, buy!"

Daylight, and the dancing dust motes.
The universe dances too; and so do our souls;
dancing with you, feet flying, they dance.
Can you see it, as I whisper in your ear?

All day and night, music,
one flute,
quiet, bright.
If it fades, we fade.

Rumi

daylight and
the dancing dust

the swan will fly at last alone

The swan will fly at last alone;
the world will seem a sideshow then.

When the leaf is taken by the wind
who can say, where it will fall?

When life's short length is ended
no more circumstance, no more attributes.

When Yama, Lord of the Dead, sends his call
the self is helpless, overwhelmed

and then you will know God.

Kabir

taken by the wind

until I am burned up

Love will not be glad
until I am burned up.
My heart is the home of love:
"Burn it!" love says.
"No, no," I protest;
"Burn it down," says love.

I will be a candle:
The more I burn, the brighter the flame.

Tonight, I will not sleep:
I will look for those lovers
whom love has driven to drink;
who burn in union with the One.

Rumi

THE HOME
OF LOVE

unlikely gold

If you are not in love
sleep on.

If you don't know that pain
in your heart,
the pain of love,
sleep on.

If your heart doesn't melt
and run, like molten copper
as you search all of alchemy
for the unlikely gold
sleep on.

I have let my mind go.
There is nothing to say.
If you are still talking,
sleep on.

Rumi

unlikely

gold

the gaze

My gaze goes straight to the heart:
I don't listen to speeches.
The heart is the truth;
words are the truth's disguise.
In all your life, how many sentences?
Too many, too many for me.
Burn the words; burn them,
make friends with fire.
Light the fire of love.
Burn the thoughts away.

Rumi

light
the fire
of love

are you looking for me?

Are you looking for me? I am next to you, on the bench.
My shoulder is leaning on yours.

When you really look for me, you'll see me at once
in the tiniest fraction of time.

The seeker asks: what is God?
I am the breath inside the breath.

Kabir

inside
the
breath

white flower

He said, I am with you always.
That means, when you look for God,
that God is the looking itself,
yes, and the thought of looking,
and the you that thinks the thought.
Always, already, all of it;
there is no outside.

A white flower grows in the silence.
Let your speech be that flower.

Rumi

all of it

love is not condescension

Love is not condescension, never
that, nor books, nor any pencil trace
on paper, no; nor in how we talk
about each other. Love is a tree

with branches reaching out to always,
with roots that come from everywhere,
and no trunk. Have you seen it?
No. You can't. Your deep desire

can't find it. The longing you feel for
love is who you are. No other.
When you become the Lover, your
longing will be like this:

a man in the ocean, holding a plank.
Soon, the plank, the man,
the sea itself, all of it, are one:
one being, one communion:

the swaying sea, the teacher,
the secret of God.

Rumi

reaching out to always

thinking about water

I've been thinking
about water. And ripples and waves.
Water moves, but it's still water.
Someone came up with a word, 'wave',
but the water didn't stop being water.

Inside each of us, there is a secret guest
whose hands tell the stars like prayer beads;
whose eyes shine. So should yours.

Kabir

the secret guest

springtime

The springtime of love has arrived.
This desert is now a garden,
the words of heaven are spoken,
the bird of the soul is in flight.
The sea fills with pearls,
the salt marsh is sweet,
that pebble is now a jewel,
the body is all made of soul.

Rumi

the
springtime
of
love

remember love

My mother holding me, looking down at me,
sometimes, smiling, she would weep.

Now, I know why. Love is strong, so strong
that it can break the cage, and for one holy moment
she disappeared from everything.

All that we do comes from that, that
taste of flying. The possibility
of being free is what moves
the body, and each cell of the body.

I wasn't able to live on earth, so I went out
alone, into the sky. I write of that journey
of becoming as free as
God.

Remember love. It will bring
all of the madness that you need
to unroll the whole of yourself
across the sky.

Mirabai

remember love

the beauty of the heart

The beauty of the heart
is what will remain:
it brings to your lips
the water of life.
In truth, it is the water,
and the jug that holds it,
and the lips that drink.

All three become one when
your talismans are broken.
This is a oneness you won't know
by thinking about it.

Rumi

what will remain

flowers for the Buddha


The winter river.
Floating on it,
flowers for the Buddha

Buson

flowers

visit www.strangeshadows.co.uk for our books, plays, songs, poems, photography, and websites

blurb

blurb.com